YOU CHOOSE
BOOKS™

THE
CIVIL RIGHTS
MOVEMENT

An Interactive History Adventure

by Heather Adamson

Consultant:
Kira Duke, Education Coordinator
National Civil Rights Museum
Memphis, Tennessee

Capstone
press®

Mankato, Minnesota

You Choose Books are published by Capstone Press,
151 Good Counsel Drive, P.O. Box 669, Mankato, Minnesota 56002.
www.capstonepress.com

Library of Congress Cataloging-in-Publication Data
Adamson, Heather, 1974–
The civil rights movement: an interactive history adventure / by Heather Adamson.
    p. cm. — (You choose books)
    Includes bibliographical references and index.
    Summary: "Describes the people and events of the U.S. civil rights movement. The reader's
choices reveal the historical details from the perspectives of a Little Rock resident, a Freedom Rider,
and a Birmingham protester" — Provided by publisher.
    ISBN-13: 978-1-4296-2345-2 (hardcover)   ISBN-13: 978-1-4296-3454-0 (softcover pbk.)
    ISBN-10: 1-4296-2345-4 (hardcover)   ISBN-10: 1-4296-3454-5 (softcover pbk.)
    1. African Americans — Civil rights — History — 20th century — Juvenile literature.
2. Civil rights movements — United States — History — 20th century — Juvenile literature.
3. United States — Race relations — Juvenile literature. I. Title. II. Series.
E185.61.A235 2009
323.1196'073 — dc22   2008034517

Editorial Credits
Angie Kaelberer, editor; Juliette Peters, set designer; Gene Bentdahl, book designer;
    Wanda Winch, photo researcher

Photo Credits
AP Images, 27, 35, 65, 69, 70, 76, 91, 92, 94, 103; AP Images/Bill Hudson, 80; AP Images/
William P. Straeter, 12; Corbis/Bettmann, cover, 18, 40, 55, 56, 83; Corbis/Jack Moebes, 38;
Courtesy, Arkansas History Commission, 29; Courtesy of the National Park Service, Little Rock
Central High School National Historic Site, 21; Getty Images Inc./Hulton Archive/Agence
France Presse/Central Press, 88; Getty Images Inc./Hulton Archive/Bob Parent, 100; Getty
Images Inc./Time & Life Pictures/Hank Walker, 6; Getty Images Inc./Time & Life Pictures/Paul
Schutzer, 61; Library of Congress, Prints & Photographs Division, NYWT&S Collection, 10,
14, 33, 46, 51; Library of Congress, Prints & Photographs Division, U.S. News & World Report
Magazine Collection, 60, 105; Library of Congress, Prints & Photographs Division, Visual
Materials from the NAACP Records, 25, 85; Wisconsin Historical Society/Fred Blackwell/
Whi2381, 44

**Note: In some of the actual incidents depicted in this book, highly offensive and
derogatory language was used. Capstone Publishing has chosen to substitute this
language in dialogue.**

1 2 3 4 5 6 14 13 12 11 10 09

TABLE OF CONTENTS

ABOUT YOUR
ADVENTURE

YOU are living in the United States during the time when African Americans aren't treated equally. Will you join in the movement to bring civil rights to all Americans?

In this book, you'll explore how the choices people made meant the difference between life and death. The events you'll experience happened to real people.

Chapter One sets the scene. Then you choose which path to read. Follow the directions at the bottom of each page. The choices you make will change your outcome. After you finish one path, go back and read the others for new perspectives and more adventures.

YOU CHOOSE the path
you take through history.

Schools for African Americans were much poorer than the schools for white students.

CHAPTER 1

A WORLD DIVIDED

Life in the southern United States is divided. Black and white people attend separate schools. They sit in separate areas in buses, restaurants, and theaters. Even drinking fountains and bathrooms are separated by race. And blacks have the lesser things. Old, broken-down schools. Seats in the back of the bus. Outhouses on the edge of town. Things have been this way for longer than you can remember.

For several hundred years, white people had forced African Americans into slavery. After the Civil War (1861–1865), life in the United States changed. The 13th Amendment to the Constitution made slavery illegal.

Turn the page.

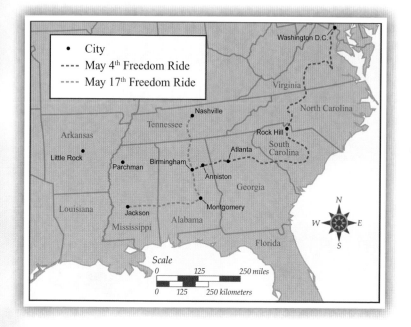

African Americans, often called Negroes, blacks, or coloreds, were free. White Southerners worried about going from owning black people to being on an equal footing with them. White people were afraid of what would happen to their towns, schools, and churches when people from a different culture joined them.

White Southerners found an answer. They decided to keep whites and blacks separate. The Supreme Court supported the idea. In an 1896 case called *Plessy vs. Ferguson*, the Court said "separate but equal" was fair. The South began a life of segregation.

Southern states also passed Jim Crow laws. These laws make it difficult for black citizens to vote, get good jobs, or a good education. The laws also keep blacks from protesting their treatment. Groups like the Ku Klux Klan terrorize and kill African Americans who defend themselves.

But African Americans believe they are equal to white citizens. By the 1950s, many are working for change. In 1954, lawyers won a big U.S. Supreme Court case, *Brown vs. Board of Education of Topeka*. The Court ruled that separate is not equal. Southern schools must accept students of all races.

Turn the page.

On December 1, 1955, Rosa Parks was arrested for refusing to give up her bus seat to a white man.

After the Supreme Court decision, even more blacks demanded civil rights. In Montgomery, Alabama, in 1955, a black woman named Rosa Parks refused to give up her bus seat to a white man. After she was arrested, blacks quit riding Montgomery buses in protest. This bus boycott lasted a little more than a year.

The civil rights movement has begun.

Both black and white Americans are fighting

for equality in schools, jobs, and public places.

What role will you play?

➤ To be involved in the desegregation of Central High School in Little Rock, Arkansas, in 1957, turn to page **13**.

➤ To join the Freedom Rides and nonviolent protests in 1961, turn to page **39**.

➤ To live in Birmingham, Alabama, in 1963, turn to page **71**.

Before 1957, only white students were allowed to attend Central High School in Little Rock.

CHAPTER 2

THE LITTLE ROCK NINE

September 2, 1957, is Labor Day in Little Rock, Arkansas. Many people are outside enjoying this last day of summer. There's a pleasant warm sun, but no one is talking about the weather. Everyone talks about school starting.

Tomorrow, nine black students will try to enroll at Central High School. This school is open to white students only. But three years ago, the Supreme Court ordered schools in the United States to desegregate. If black children are equal to white children, they must go to the same schools.

13

Turn the page.

Arkansas Governor Orval Faubus was against desegregating Central High.

It is not hard for you to see why black students want to attend Central. It is one of the most beautiful schools in the country. Its students receive an excellent education.

The desegregation has been planned for two years. But now that the day is finally here, people are uneasy. The Mother's League and some local church groups plan to march in the morning against desegregation.

The minister from your church called earlier. He asked if you would like to join a small group of people. They will escort the black children to school tomorrow.

You are not sure what you should do. You like your city. You have a good life. Will desegregation make things better? Or will it divide the city and lead to violence?

After supper, you turn on the TV. Governor Orval Faubus is speaking. Faubus is against forced desegregation. He believes it will cause riots. Faubus plans to send the National Guard to Central tomorrow. He says the soldiers will "preserve the peace and avoid violence." But you're not sure that's what will happen.

In the morning, you learn desegregation has been delayed until tomorrow. You are glad to avoid making a decision for another day.

Turn the page.

At work, your boss tells you he won't have any part of desegregation. You know you will probably lose your job if you escort the black students. After work, you are barely in the door of your house when the phone rings.

It's your minister. He says, "Meet at 12th Street and Park Avenue tomorrow morning if you want to join the escort group." A moment later, the phone rings again. A friend asks you to march against desegregation. She says, "We can't let the federal government decide what's best for Little Rock."

→ To protest desegregation, go to page 17.

→ To support desegregation, turn to page 22.

You decide to protest against desegregation. The city shouldn't have to change its way of life. You go downtown on September 4. Hundreds of whites line the streets. Some carry signs that read "We won't integrate" and "No Negroes."

You stand with the rows of people across from the school. The grounds are surrounded by hundreds of National Guard soldiers with guns. It looks like a war zone. A few people parade down the street with their signs.

Then one black girl arrives at the edge of the property. She is wearing a freshly ironed white blouse and checkered skirt. No one is with her. She clutches her books close as she tries to walk behind the line of soldiers to the school door. But the guard points her to the crowd. It's clear that the soldiers aren't there to help her.

Turn the page.

People screamed at Elizabeth Eckford as she tried to enter the school.

The girl crosses the road. She has to walk past you to get to the school. The crowd backs up. You give her space to walk. The crowd follows right behind her. They start to yell. You join in shouting, "2, 4, 6, 8, we ain't gonna integrate."

The soldiers raise their guns when the girl tries to enter the school. The sun glints on the bayonets on the end of the guns. The soldiers are blocking the girl from entering the school.

This stirs up the crowd. If the girl doesn't get in the school, the world will see that Little Rock can't be pushed around. The shouting grows angrier. The crowd moves closer to the black girl. People scream right into her ears as she walks. "Coloreds don't belong here!" "Go home, Negro!" "Lynch her! Lynch her!" An old woman spits in the girl's face.

You can see the girl wants to get out of here. She walks quickly to the bus stop down the block. The crowd chases after her. You know she must be scared.

➤ To make sure the girl is too scared to come back tomorrow, turn to page **20**.

➤ To help the girl, turn to page **21**.

The girl sits on the bench at the bus stop. Someone yells, "Find a rope. Let's string her up a tree!" A group of white reporters from out of town shield the bench from the crowd. "Get out of the way!" you yell at them. One of the reporters sits down next to the girl and puts an arm around her. "Don't let them see you cry," he tells her.

A white woman pushes her way through the crowd. She tells the crowd to leave the girl alone. Then she takes the girl's hand and helps her escape the crowd. A few minutes later, the other black students arrive. They are quickly chased away as well. There's no way they will dare come back tomorrow.

*Turn to page **24**.*

Grace Lorch (left) tried to protect Elizabeth Eckford (center) from the crowd.

The girl sits alone on the bus stop bench. A white reporter pushes through the crowd and sits next to the girl. He puts his arm around her. The crowd shouts at him. You know if you help, the angry crowd may attack you.

But the girl is just a kid. Someone must help her. You quietly worm your way through the crowd. A white woman is now scolding the crowd for their treatment of the girl. You and the woman take the girl's hands and quickly lead her away from the crowd.

Turn to page 23.

You decide it is time for the city to move forward with desegregation. You know you may get hurt or lose your job. But your minister is right. Some people need to stand for peace.

On the morning of September 4, you head downtown to 12th Street. That's where the black students and escorts are supposed to meet. As you get near Central High, your stomach sinks. A huge crowd of white people and soldiers are in front of the school. They are following one black girl who is trying to get into the school.

You don't know where the other students are. You decide to try to help the girl. You struggle through the shouting crowd. The girl heads for a bus stop bench. "Lynch her! Lynch her!" the crowd roars. You can't believe that they're screaming about hanging a young girl. A white woman in the crowd starts to scold the people who are harassing the girl.

"What's your name?" you ask the girl.

"I'm Elizabeth . . . Elizabeth Eckford," she replies.

The white woman says her name is Grace Lorch. You tell Elizabeth you will call her a taxi. You walk to a nearby drugstore, but the owner shuts the door. He doesn't want the crowd to follow you to his store. Other shop owners also shut their doors as they see you approach. You look around. The bus is coming up the street. You, Grace, and Elizabeth quickly get on the bus as it stops. You pay the fares and stay with Elizabeth until you're sure she's safe. You hope violence has not erupted all over the city.

Turn the page.

Over the next few days, the story is national news. The black students will not try to enter the school again until the National Guard leaves. President Dwight Eisenhower tells Governor Faubus to follow the desegregation order. On Friday, September 20, Judge Ronald Davies orders Faubus to remove the troops. Faubus reluctantly agrees.

At work on Saturday, your boss calls all the employees into his office. "I hear those Negroes are going to try to get in the school again on Monday morning," he says. "If you need to be late to help keep them out, you won't miss any pay. But if I catch word of you helping them, you won't be working here anymore."

At church on Sunday, your minister asks you again to help escort the black children. "If you are willing, meet at Daisy Bates' house."

Daisy Bates (row two, second from right) helped organize the desegregation effort.

Daisy is a civil rights leader. She's president of the Arkansas chapter of the National Association for the Advancement of Colored People (NAACP).

➤ To keep the students out, turn to page **26**.

➤ To try to stay out of trouble, turn to page **32**.

➤ To escort the students, turn to page **34**.

As you drive toward Central on Monday morning, you see groups of white people heading downtown. There must be thousands of people crowded around the school. Some stand ready with sticks and bottles to throw at the students. Some seem to only want to watch. You park and make your way to a place where you can see.

There's no National Guard today. Only the city police. You wait a while. Nothing happens. Every time a car drives up to the school, the crowd pushes ahead, hoping it is the black students. Maybe they decided not to come.

Just then, you see a car pull up around the back of the school. You see dark-skinned people inside it. The crowd rushes to the car. You run too. But it is not the children and their parents. It is a group of black reporters. A few people tell them to run. "No Negroes at Central — not even reporters!"

National Guard officers first blocked the black students but later escorted them.

You look behind you and see the police open a side door on the school. The black students are quietly walking into the school. "They're getting in!" someone shouts. No one can believe it. People curse and scream.

Many people in the crowd are looking for another target for their anger. They turn to the black reporters.

⟶ To go after the reporters, turn to page 28.

⟶ To leave before a riot breaks out, turn to page 32.

You feel frustrated. You join the people chasing the black reporters. Three of the reporters run to safety as quickly as they can. But one of the reporters doesn't run. He walks slowly, carrying his hat in his hand. A white man kicks him in the stomach and tells him to run away. The reporter wipes his forehead and keeps walking. The crowd grows angrier that he won't run and he won't fight. They punch and slap him. He falls down, gets up, and keeps walking.

"You'd better run," you tell the reporter. A man comes running toward the two of you with a large brick in his hand. But he doesn't have enough room to throw it.

➤ *To move out of the way so the man can hit the reporter with the brick, go to page **29**.*

➤ *To stop the man from throwing the brick, turn to page **31**.*

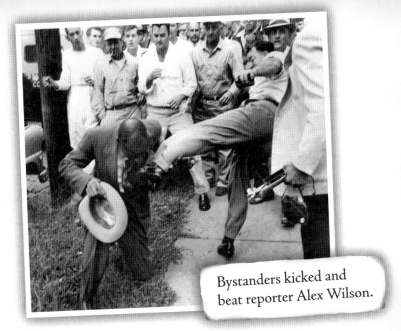

Bystanders kicked and beat reporter Alex Wilson.

You move out of the way and yell, "Hit him."
The man draws back his arm to throw the brick.
"No!" screams another man in the crowd. He
grabs the arm of the man with the brick. The
brick falls to the ground. You pick it up and
plunk it as hard as you can against the reporter's
head. He falls to the ground.

A few minutes later, the reporter gets up. He
is still holding his hat in his hand as he walks to
his car and drives away.

Turn the page.

Later, you learn that the reporter's name is Alex Wilson. Wilson survives, but is in poor health. He dies in 1960, likely from injuries related to the beating. Central High is eventually desegregated in spite of your hatred. In time, blacks and whites even sit together on the Little Rock city board of directors.

THE END

To follow another path, turn to page 11.
To read the conclusion, turn to page 101.

"No!" you scream. You grab the arm of the man trying to throw the brick. The brick falls to the ground. But someone else quickly picks it up and thunks it against the reporter's head. The reporter falls to the ground, still holding his hat. A few minutes later, he gets up and walks to his car. Later, you learn that his name is Alex Wilson. Wilson dies three years later, likely from injuries caused by this beating.

Central High and the rest of the Little Rock schools eventually desegregate. Years later, you feel bad about what you did in 1957. You know you acted in fear. You try to find those you hurt and apologize to them. You do your best to raise your own children to respect people of all races.

THE END

To follow another path, turn to page 11.
To read the conclusion, turn to page 101.

You are glad to be at home and away from the crowd. You sit down in the living room and turn on the TV. The black students made it safely in the side door, but outside, the crowd boils. The city police try to keep things under control. But the people swarm, yell, and scream. They throw bottles and bricks.

That evening President Eisenhower calls in federal soldiers and takes control of the National Guard. The next day, the black students walk through Central's front doors. Armed guards escort them.

The students use military escorts for the rest of the year. At school, white students trip, shove, and taunt them. Some teachers refuse to come near them. The city stays divided.

This sign in front of Central High is incorrect. Arkansas' governor closed the schools.

THIS SCHOOL **CLOSED** BY ORDER OF THE FEDERAL GOVERMENT

At the end of the school year, Governor Faubus closes the three public high schools in Little Rock to avoid more desegregation. Only private high schools remain open. Many students quit school. Others move away to attend school in other cities and states. After a year without school, Central High is finally desegregated peacefully. It's just a small step toward equality.

THE END

To follow another path, turn to page 11.
To read the conclusion, turn to page 101.

When you get to Daisy Bates' house, your minister is outside among a small group of people. "Thank you for coming," he tells you. "There's someone here I'd like you to meet."

A tall black man standing next to your minister holds out his hand to you. "I'm Alex Wilson," he says. "I'm here to cover the story for the *Memphis Tri-State Defender* newspaper."

As you shake Wilson's hand, Bates comes out the door. The nine students follow her. You smile at them as they climb into two station wagons.

"Thank you for coming," Bates tells you, "but the city police will escort us to school today. That way, it will be safer for everyone." She looks at Wilson and three other black reporters standing nearby. "The police will take the students through a back door into the school."

The students gathered in front of Daisy Bates' house before school on September 25, 1957.

Turn the page.

The reporters thank Bates for the information and drive off. The students follow close behind. You are relieved that you didn't have to face a mob today.

As you walk to your car, you see two of your coworkers across the street. They glare at you. You know they will tell your boss.

When you get to work, your boss fires you. But that is not the worst. On the news that night, you see the crowd beating Alex Wilson in front of the school. They even hit him on the side of the head with a brick! He's able to get up and walk away. You pray that he'll be all right.

In the next few days, you start to get phone calls from strangers. "Better keep an eye on your children, Negro-lover!" the callers taunt before hanging up.

The calls start to come more often. One night, you hear a huge crash from downstairs. Someone throws a brick through your front window and drives away.

You are afraid the next time it might be a stick of dynamite. You decide to move your family away from Little Rock. You are surprised at how much trying to do the right thing has cost you. But you aren't sorry.

A few years later, you hear that Alex Wilson died, probably due to injuries he received that day. You are sad to hear the news, but proud that you supported him and others in the fight for equality.

THE END

To follow another path, turn to page 11.
To read the conclusion, turn to page 101.

In February 1960, four students held a sit-in at the Woolworth's lunch counter in Greensboro, North Carolina.

CHAPTER 3

RIDING FOR FREEDOM

"It's going to be the young people," says your roommate at Ohio's Central State College. "Students like us will change things."

It's spring 1961. Your roommate is talking about how blacks and whites are not treated equally in the South. He has just returned from a workshop in Tennessee. He says there's a peaceful protest movement going on. During the last year, you've heard about students "sitting in" at lunch counters. The students find places that serve only whites. They sit at the stools and tables until the business agrees to serve black customers.

Turn the page.

From left: James Farmer, Ralph Abernathy, Dr. Martin Luther King Jr., and John Lewis helped organize the student protests.

You believe all people are equal. You want to learn more. Your roommate tells you about a student group called the Student Nonviolent Coordinating Committee (SNCC). You join the group. John Lewis, Diane Nash, and other SNCC members are planning more training workshops. You can't wait to attend one of them.

Back at college, your roommate asks you to come to Atlanta, Georgia, with him the next weekend. He's going to a sit-in at a drugstore lunch counter.

You want to work for change, but you're not sure that you're ready. Sitting sounds easy enough, but what if there is violence? Some students have been arrested. And one of the lawyers for the students, Z. Alexander Looby, had his house bombed.

➤ *To wait for more training before you start protesting, turn to page 42.*

➤ *To take part in the sit-in, turn to page 43.*

You decide you need to be more prepared before becoming a protester. You go to a workshop. There, you practice staying calm as people shout at you and spit on you.

You learn that if enough people are arrested, the jails fill up. When the jails are full, officials have no choice but to give in to the demands. If you are arrested, you need to stay in jail as long as possible before getting bailed out.

The SNCC is asking for "Freedom Riders." In 1960, the Supreme Court ordered interstate buses and stations to desegregate. So far, the South has ignored the court's ruling. People of all ages and races are needed to test the segregation rules. You know it could be violent. Maybe you should start with a lunch counter sit-in instead.

➜ *To take part in a sit-in, go to page **43**.*
➜ *To join the Freedom Riders, turn to page **46**.*

How hard can it be to sit at a counter all day? You go down to Atlanta for the sit-in. One by one, each protester will buy something at the store and then sit at the lunch counter. You buy some pencils and a pack of spearmint chewing gum. It isn't long before all the seats at the lunch counter are taken.

The servers ignore everyone and try to pretend they don't hear the students asking for a cup of coffee. They fill the napkin holders and wipe the dishes instead.

Soon a few angry white people enter the store. "Go home, Negroes and Negro-lovers!" yells a woman. A man spits on a few of the students. Another crushes a burning cigarette into the arm of the boy next to you. You don't move. You can't react to their abuse. Then a man grabs your collar and pours itching powder down your shirt. "See how long you can sit now!"

Turn the page.

Sit-in participants didn't react when people poured ketchup and mustard on them.

You feel the powder tickle and burn your back. You chew your gum and stay calm. You try to sit as still as you can. About an hour later, the police come in and tell you to leave. You look at the other students. No one gets up. One of the police officers tells the store manager to close the store for the day. Some students cheer as the manager brings out his closed sign.

Since no one is sure if the store will even reopen on Monday, you and your roommate head back to school. Your roommate seems a little disappointed no one was arrested. You are just happy to have survived your first sit-in. But you have a newfound energy for civil rights protests. You know you want to play a bigger role.

At school, you find out there is a need for people to help desegregate bus transportation in the South. You sign up to be a Freedom Rider.

Turn to page 52.

Freedom Riders knew they were putting their lives at risk when they left Washington, D.C.

You know being a Freedom Rider is dangerous, but you believe in the cause. Dr. Martin Luther King Jr., Reverend Ralph Abernathy, Diane Nash, and James Farmer planned the protests. The black riders will sit in the front of the bus, in the seats reserved for whites. The white riders will sit in the back. At each stop, the white riders will sit in the colored waiting rooms and use the colored restrooms. The black riders will sit in the whites-only waiting rooms and use the white restrooms.

No matter what happens or how violent it gets, Freedom Riders must stay calm and not fight back. No one is sure what to expect. You know there's a possibility you could be killed. Many of the other riders are making out wills and last letters to their families. You are not sure if you are ready to take part in the protests.

→ To take part in the first ride, turn to page **48**.

→ To continue training before joining the ride, turn to page **52**.

You are one of the 13 riders in the first group. Your journey begins May 4 in Washington, D.C. The bus makes stops in Virginia, North Carolina, South Carolina, and Georgia. There's some shouting and a scuffle or two, but luckily no large-scale violence.

At most of the stops, the riders all get off the bus. The whites go to the colored restrooms, and the blacks go to the white restrooms. A few people shout at you, "Hey, go where you belong!" A lunch counter worker says he's out of coffee, although there's a full pot on the stove.

The biggest incident is in Rock Hill, South Carolina. A group of about 20 angry white men are waiting in the station when you arrive. John Lewis gets off the bus first and goes to use the white restroom. The mob starts hitting him with their fists.

You follow close behind John. A few people in the crowd slap your face and kick your shins. The police break up the fight. You continue your journey with just a few small bruises.

Now you are waiting in Atlanta. It's Sunday, May 14. The next leg of your trip takes you to the most segregated, violent parts of the South. The group will follow two staggered routes. One bus will leave an hour before the other. No one is sure which bus will be the safest.

➔ *To go on the early bus through Anniston, Alabama, turn to page 50.*

➔ *To take the later bus to Birmingham, Alabama, turn to page 54.*

The ride to Anniston is quiet. The terminal is closed when your bus arrives. Before anyone can decide what to do, about 200 angry people run out from behind the building.

A man lies down in front of the bus so it can't drive away. The crowd throws rocks at the bus. A window shatters as you crouch under your seat. The crowd beats on the bus with pipes, baseball bats, and chains.

"Cowards!" the crowd chants. Finally the police arrive, and the crowd backs away. The bus tries to speed off, but its tires have been slashed. A parade of angry white drivers quickly catches up to the bus. Just a few miles from the city limits, the bus can go no farther. It must pull over.

The bus driver jumps out and runs away. The crowd starts to rock the bus. "Get out here and take what you've got coming!" Your heart thumps in fear.

Angry whites firebombed a Freedom Riders bus in Anniston, Alabama.

Suddenly a firebomb smashes through the window. The air fills with smoke. You can't breathe. You hear someone yell, "Burn them alive!" There's a small explosion. You and the others manage to get out the back door.

You are crawling away from the flaming bus when a white man runs up to you. "Are you OK?" he asks. You look up at him for help. He grins and smashes you in the face with a baseball bat. Everything goes black. You wake a few hours later in the emergency room of the Anniston hospital.

Turn to page 68.

You have a few important things to do before heading out on a Freedom Ride. You finish more training in nonviolence. You know that you face danger during the rides. You write a will and letters to your friends and family to be mailed if you are killed.

You will be a replacement rider. Mobs of angry whites, many of them members of the Ku Klux Klan, beat the first riders. They are too injured to continue. Your group will start its journey in Birmingham, Alabama, where the last group was stopped. You will travel about 85 miles to Montgomery, Alabama.

On Saturday, May 20, you board the bus in Birmingham. For safety, Alabama state police cars drive in front and in back of the bus. A police helicopter hovers in the sky. In Montgomery, city police are scheduled to be at the bus station to protect you.

As you reach Montgomery, you notice that the state police cars and the helicopter are no longer with you. The town is still and quiet. "Where is everyone?" you ask as the bus pulls into the deserted station. You get your answer as a large mob appears. Men gather at the front door of the bus. They're armed with chains, bats, pipes, and hammers. You know they are probably members of the Ku Klux Klan. The police officers you were promised are nowhere to be seen.

"Let's jump out the back!" someone says. If you get away, you could come back tomorrow to continue the ride. Or should you go through the front door and face the mob? Maybe they'll be less angry if you don't try to run.

➻ To escape out the back door, turn to page **56**.
➻ To go out the front door, turn to page **57**.

As your bus arrives for a brief stop in Anniston, the station is quiet. You get off and buy a few sandwiches at the lunch counter without any problems. Just before the bus pulls away for Birmingham, a gang of white men boards the bus. "Negroes get to the back where you belong!" the largest man shouts. No one moves.

One of the men pulls you out of your seat and begins to beat you. Other riders are also punched and kicked. Most of the riders are unconscious. The men drag the black riders to the back and the whites to the front. The bus driver then starts driving to Birmingham.

By the time the bus pulls into Birmingham, you have regained consciousness and try to gather strength for what waits at the station. The white men who attacked you jump off the bus.

James Peck was one of the Freedom Riders beaten at the Birmingham station.

As you enter the station, you start walking to the "wrong" waiting room. The crowd surrounds you. It's all a blur as white men with chains, pipes, and bats chase and beat you.

You see another Freedom Rider fall down. You try to get over to him to help him up. Each time, you are knocked down again. Then, you look up and see the crowd running away. You and the other riders get up and check on each other. You're bleeding and bruised, but alive. When the police arrive, they take you to a hospital.

Turn to page 68.

You decide to try to escape the mob. You move toward the back of the bus. But before you can get out, you see your friend Jim Zwerg walk to the front of the bus. He is a young white student. He will surely be beaten severely for being a "Negro-lover." You will not let him go out there alone. All the riders turn and follow Jim.

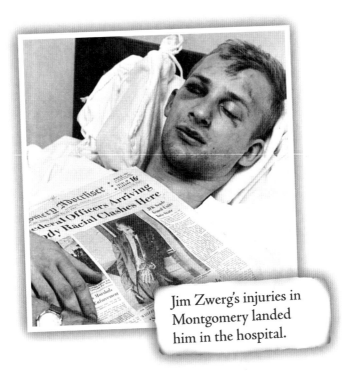

Jim Zwerg's injuries in Montgomery landed him in the hospital.

Jim Zwerg is the first off the bus. As he steps out the front door into the mob, the men grab him. At first they don't seem to notice the rest of you. Will they only attack Jim? WHACK! You feel a piece of metal hit you in the back. You see a couple riders heading for a side street. You don't know where it goes. It might be a chance to get away alive. You see a few other riders trying to get through the mob to Jim and make their way into the terminal.

→ To go down the side street, turn to page **58**.

→ To try to help Jim, turn to page **67**.

A hammer hits you in the leg as you run toward the side street. A group of angry men chase you. "You won't get away from us, boy!" they scream at you. This route is a dead end. You are pinned at a railing above a parking ramp. The mob is coming.

"We have to jump!" you yell at the other riders. They nod. You all gather your courage and leap 15 feet to the cement parking lot below. The landing is rough, but everyone is OK. You get up and escape by hiding in a nearby post office.

Moments later, the police finally arrive. They jokingly ask the riders why they were beating each other. Later, you learn the Ku Klux Klan made a deal with the city police. Klan members had at least 15 minutes to attack the Freedom Riders before police would arrive.

The next evening, you attend a rally in Montgomery in support of the Freedom Riders. It's at Reverend Ralph Abernathy's church, First Baptist. About 1,200 people show up. Federal marshals protect the church.

As civil rights leader Dr. Martin Luther King Jr. speaks, several thousand angry white people surround the church. They throw bottles at the marshals. The marshals throw tear gas at the mob. The tear gas gets inside the church.

You choke and gasp from the tear gas. Your eyes burn and fill with tears. The skin inside your nose feels like it is crawling. You wonder if you will die in this building.

Turn the page.

U. S. Attorney General Robert F. Kennedy supported the civil rights protesters.

At 3:00 in the morning, King calls U.S. Attorney General Robert F. Kennedy to ask for help. Kennedy calls Alabama Governor John Patterson and convinces him to send the National Guard to break up the crowd.

As the mob leaves, state troopers escort you out of the church. You know more than ever that the rides must continue.

National Guard troops protected the riders from Montgomery to Jackson.

On May 24, you are one of 27 Freedom Riders heading for Jackson, Mississippi. National Guard troops escort you to the station at Jackson. At the station, police let you off the bus and allow you to walk through the terminal. Then they escort you into paddy wagons. You are arrested and convicted of trespassing.

After a couple weeks in the Jackson jail, you're transferred to Parchman State Penitentiary. It's one of the roughest jails in the South.

Turn the page.

You enter the maximum security wing. You see a long row of small cell rooms, each covered with metal bars. The cells look out at a blank wall that has a few high windows at the top.

The guards order you to strip naked. They give you a T-shirt and a pair of boxer shorts. Then they hand you a small cup, a Bible, and a toothbrush before locking you in your cell. "We had better not hear you singing any of those protest songs," they warn you. But some of the riders decide to sing freedom songs anyway.

➥ *If you keep quiet, go to page* **63**.

➥ *If you join the singing, turn to page* **64**.

You decide you don't have the strength to protest in jail. But when you hear the others singing, "Keep Your Eyes on the Prize," you are inspired. You can even hear a loud, clear voice bouncing off the metal walls of "the hole." The hole is a 6-foot metal box in the prison basement used to punish prisoners. In the hole, there is no light. Prisoners are not given any food or water. If someone in the hole can sing, you can too. You add your voice to the others.

Turn the page.

"Keep your eyes on the prize," you sing with the other jailed Freedom Riders. The warden comes and says, "Shut up or we'll take your toothbrushes." You keep singing. The guards take the toothbrushes.

You keep singing. "Next, it's your Bibles." You keep singing as the guards take the Bibles. Then they take your mattresses and bedding.

The warden is angry that you are still singing. He yells, "Stop singing or else!" Then the guards remove the screens on the windows high up in the hallway. Hundreds of mosquitoes fly into the cells. Soon your arms and legs are covered with stinging red welts from the mosquitoes' bites. You try to keep singing.

Freedom Riders were jailed in the maximum security unit at Parchman State Penitentiary.

Turn the page.

Later in the evening, the guards come to your cells. "Shut up!" they shout. You and the others keep singing. The guards use fire hoses to spray the pesticide DDT into the cells. It burns your skin and your eyes.

In the morning, more Freedom Riders arrive. Every day, more riders join you. It keeps up your spirits. You know you will have to spend 40 days in jail. That's the maximum amount of time you can serve under the charge.

Finally, you are released and sent home. By the end of the summer, the Freedom Rides end. Most bus stations have been desegregated. But more importantly, you have paved the way for peaceful protests. Many more people are inspired to peacefully risk their lives for freedom.

THE END

To follow another path, turn to page 11.
To read the conclusion, turn to page 101.

You put your hands in front of your face and run into the crowd. A chain whips across your arms. You hear a cracking noise as a bat thumps your spine. You fall to the ground. You feel heavy shoes and boots kicking and stomping your body. It all goes dark.

You wake up in the back of a car with a cloth around your head. You wonder if you are being taken to be hanged from a tree somewhere. Then you hear a friendly voice say, "We'll get you to a doctor."

Turn the page.

You are badly hurt, but you want to continue the ride if you can. However, the organizers decide that you should go home to recover. Other Freedom Riders will take your place. You're disappointed, but glad that the mission will continue.

THE END

To follow another path, turn to page 11.
To read the conclusion, turn to page 101.

Freedom Rides continued into August 1961.

Many people considered Birmingham, Alabama, the most segregated city in the South.

CHAPTER 4

BOMBINGHAM, 1963

It's spring 1963. Across the South, many changes are taking place for black people. Buses and lunch counters have been desegregated. Last year, civil rights leader Medgar Evers helped enroll black student James Meredith at the University of Mississippi. It took U.S. marshals, the National Guard, and the army to get Meredith in the building. Still, there's finally a black man going to Ole Miss!

But in your hometown of Birmingham, Alabama, things haven't improved. White people don't want anything to do with you and other blacks.

Turn the page.

The town closed all the public parks and swimming pools so they wouldn't have to desegregate them. There's not even Little League baseball. The whites are afraid the government might make the black and white children play together. But maybe things are about to change.

Dr. Martin Luther King Jr. has started Project C in the city. "C" stands for "confrontation." King wants there to be so many protests in Birmingham that the whole country takes notice. It is both exciting and scary. If a black-owned business starts doing well, the Ku Klux Klan burns it down. It happens so often that people call your city "Bombingham." Project C might bring more trouble before it brings change.

Your parents plan to join the protests. You are only 16, but you think you're old enough to take part as well.

"I should go instead of you," says your father.

"Dad, if you're arrested, you could lose your job," you reply. "How would we buy food?"

"You're old enough to get a job, son. If anything ever happened to me, you would take care of the family, right?"

"Yes, sir."

"Well," Mom says, "if he's old enough to take care of the family, he's old enough to decide for himself if he wants to protest."

➻ To skip the protests, turn to page **74**.

➻ To represent your family at the protests, turn to page **80**.

The more you think about it, the more you worry about being hurt during the protests. You tell Dad you don't want to march.

"That's all right, son," he replies. "It's my job as the head of the family to go." He makes you promise again to take care of the family if he is hurt or killed. You agree, but you pray nothing will happen to him.

It is early afternoon on Palm Sunday, April 7. Your father and others will march from your church, Sixteenth Street Baptist, to the city hall steps. Yesterday about 30 people were arrested for their "disorderly conduct" of praying and singing.

You stand back with a bunch of boys to watch the march. You see Leroy Allen, a neighbor boy a few years older than you. Leroy is walking the other way.

"Leroy, come with us," you call to him.

"I don't want to be arrested," he replies.

"We're just watching," you tell him.

"OK," says Leroy, "I have to catch the bus to work soon anyway." There is a small crowd of people watching from a distance. Your father and the group march calmly up the street to the steps of city hall. Then the police, their dogs, and the police wagons arrive. The officers push Dad into the back of a wagon.

Leroy decides to get a closer view on his way to his bus stop. The officers yell, "Get back!" Leroy turns around, but Police Commissioner Bull Connor tells the officers to let loose the dogs. The officer lets go of the leash. "Sic him!" he tells the dog.

Turn the page.

Birmingham police ordered their dogs to attack the protesters.

The German shepherd attacks. It grabs
Leroy's backside and then his leg. Its jaws close
down on his arm. Leroy tries to fight off the dog,
but four police officers knock him to the ground.
As the officers hold Leroy down, another police
dog comes and bites him again. Then, the officers
handcuff Leroy and throw him roughly into a
police wagon.

→ To try to help Leroy, go to page 77.

→ To run home, turn to page 78.

"Let my friend go!" you yell at the police officers as you run toward the paddy wagon. "He wasn't bothering anyone!"

"Oh, really?" a large police officer spits at you. "You must be a hoodlum just like him. We need to get all of you off the streets." The officer grabs you by the arm and tosses you into the paddy wagon beside Leroy. You're headed to jail.

Turn to page 79.

You run home to tell Mom what has happened. The phone rings often through the night and the next day. You learn that Leroy is OK, but in jail. You also learn that Dad may be in jail longer than you thought. The movement doesn't have as much money as it needs to bail everyone out. Plus, Dad's boss calls to say that he is fired for missing work.

Turn to page 92.

Leroy sits beside you in the wagon, bleeding and moaning from the pain. "It's OK, Leroy," you tell him. "We'll get you help soon." But you don't know who is going to help him at the jail.

At the jail, you're thrown into a cell with Leroy and several other protestors. You don't know where your dad is, and you're hungry and scared. A jail officer takes Leroy to the hospital for treatment and then brings him back to the jail.

The next morning, a guard comes and grabs you. "You're out of here, boy," he growls at you. "Make sure you don't come back here again."

You're being released because of your age. Dad and Leroy have to stay, though. You run home as quickly as you can.

Turn to page 92.

About 950 children took part in the first day of the Children's Crusade.

The Project C movement is planning a march called the Children's Crusade. Leaders are asking Birmingham schoolchildren to protest and be arrested. The children can fill the jails, and their parents won't have to lose their jobs. Your parents say it's all right for you to participate, but they worry about you being hurt. "Let's see how things go this first day before you join in," your mother tells you.

On May 2, the first wave of 50 children marches from the park to city hall. They range in age from 6 to 18, but most are older than 10. The children sing a peace song and walk calmly, two by two. As they get to the steps, they are arrested. Another wave of children begins marching from the park. Soon the police wagons are full. The police bring school buses to drive the children to jail. By the end of the afternoon, about 950 kids have been arrested, but no one has been hurt. Mom agrees that the children's march is safe. You can join the protests tomorrow.

The next day, you dress in nice clothes and comb your hair. You know you are supposed to be at your best as you are arrested. What you don't know is that the jails are full. Police Commissioner Bull Connor has decided he must keep the protesters from reaching city hall.

Turn the page.

You and the other kids walk to the park, singing "We Shall Overcome." Suddenly, four fire trucks pull up. The firefighters use their water hoses like cannons as they blast down children. Some start to run. Others keep marching.

You move forward. The blast of water hits you in the chest and knocks you to the pavement. The water tears open the side of your pants with its power. You grab onto a nearby tree and hold tight. The water cuts open your shirt and rips off the skin on your back. You are bleeding and hurt. You don't know if you can make it past the water hoses to city hall.

→ To continue your protest, go to page **83**.
→ To get help for your injuries, turn to page **84**.

Birmingham firefighters turned their hoses on the young protesters.

You run from your tree and try to duck behind a store. The hoses continue to blast. The water feels like a club when it hits you. You see a group of kids huddled in the street in a tight circle. They inch their way forward, holding each other up. You make your way to that group. The firefighters bring bigger hoses. They aim the water at the kids on the edge. The water knocks down a boy and rolls him along the street. The rest of the group doesn't let go of each other. The firefighters try to pick apart the group. Finally they turn off the hoses, and you run home.

Turn the page.

Your mother tells you she is proud of you for not fighting back. She helps you take off your wet, bloody clothes and puts ointment on your back. The next day, pictures of the brave children trying to march to city hall fill the newspaper. The pictures appear in newspapers all over the country.

Protests continue over the next few days. The white people in Birmingham are embarrassed. They don't want the world to think all they do is hurt black children. City leaders agree to desegregate lunch counters, hire more black workers, and let the protesters out of jail.

You are glad about all of this, but your father lost his job for supporting the protests. "If I don't have work soon," Dad says, "I'll have to go stay with my brother in Georgia. They'll need crop pickers up that way for peaches and such."

Medgar Evers was assassinated in Mississippi on June 12, 1963.

You know you will need to take care of the house if he goes. And you know that crop picking is hard work that doesn't pay well. As if the idea of Dad having to leave the family wasn't bad enough, you learn terrible news.

"They got Medgar Evers!" Mom cries as she runs into the room. "I heard it on the radio. The Ku Klux Klan shot him last night in his own driveway in Mississippi."

Turn the page.

"It's almost enough to make a black man not want to do anything to be noticed," Dad says. You think about how hard Evers worked for equality. Now he is gone.

But your family is not quitting the fight. In August, there is going to be a rally in Washington, D.C. The rally is called the March on Washington for Jobs and Freedom. People will march from the Washington Monument to the Lincoln Memorial. It is important to get as many people to the rally as possible. But with so many civil rights leaders in the same place, it could be dangerous. Everyone is wondering if it will be a safe place to bring children.

Your parents say you can decide. You can go to the march. Or you can stay home and take care of the neighborhood kids so more adults can go.

➤ *To go to the march, go to page* **87**.

➤ *To stay home and babysit, turn to page* **94**.

You decide to go to the march with your parents. Your younger brother and sister will stay with your cousins. Northern churches are sending down school buses to pick up riders in Birmingham. Mom cooks two hams and packs them in a pail with biscuits. There may not be any restaurants that serve blacks along the way.

You get to Washington, D.C., early in the morning of August 28. It is an amazing sight. There are more people than you have ever seen. White people are talking to black people and smiling. You wonder if life could ever be like this in Birmingham.

More than 250,000 people crowd near the Lincoln Memorial. Even though it is hot and crowded, everyone is excited. Singers like Bob Dylan and Marian Anderson perform. Civil rights leaders speak.

Turn the page.

Dr. Martin Luther King Jr. gave his famous "I have a dream" speech at the march.

In the evening, Dr. King gives a powerful speech. "I have a dream that my four little children will one day live in a nation where they will not be judged by the color of their skin, but by the content of their character," he says. He ends by saying he dreams that one day, people of all races and religions will join hands and sing, "Free at last, free at last. Thank God Almighty, we are free at last." You go home hopeful that freedom will come to your city.

The march is all that anyone talks about for the next few weeks. On September 15, Sunday school is starting again at your church, Sixteenth Street Baptist. To celebrate, the youth are leading part of the services.

You have some free time between services. Some kids are getting ready in the basement of the church. Other kids are playing outside on the lawn. You are not sure if you should stay inside and keep clean or if you should go outside for some fresh air.

➻ *To go outside, turn to page* **90**.

➻ *To stay in the church, turn to page* **96**.

You go outside to meet your friends. As you head out onto the grass, BOOM! The church explodes from a dynamite blast. Glass flies everywhere. You see smoke coming out of the broken windows. Screams of children rip through the air.

You see children trying to get out of the church, and you race to help them. Many children are bleeding and covered in glass. You help lead them away from the building to safety. Many kids are taken to the hospital.

You find out later in the day that four of the girls in the basement died. Eleven-year-old Denise "Niecie" McNair was one of them. She was a friend of your little sister's. You are angry.

The bomb left a huge hole in the Sixteenth Street Baptist Church.

Announcers on the radio and TV say everyone should stay inside for their safety. But you really want to find your friends. You just want to know that they are OK.

→ To stay home, turn to page 97.

→ To check on your friends, turn to page 98.

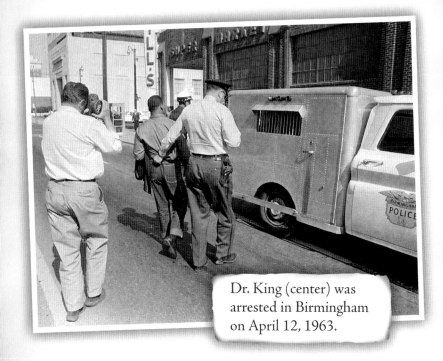

Dr. King (center) was arrested in Birmingham on April 12, 1963.

On Friday, April 12, Dr. King marches to the courthouse and is arrested. In jail, he writes a letter explaining his reasons for supporting nonviolent protests. The letter is published in newspapers all over the country.

It takes many more protests, but eventually the downtown businesses give in. They desegregate the lunch counters and hire more black workers. The success in Birmingham inspires other people in the South. Blacks in other cities start using protest marches to fight for their rights.

When Dad is released, no one will hire him because of his arrest. You quit school and get a job at a restaurant to help the family. You take classes at night. You're determined to graduate from college and spend the rest of your life working for equality.

THE END

To follow another path, turn to page 11.
To read the conclusion, turn to page 101.

Both black and white citizens participated in the March on Washington.

You decide to stay home to take care of your younger brother and sister and some of the neighborhood children. It is a big job to care for all the kids, but you know it is important.

In the evening, you feed the kids their supper and then turn on the TV. You see hundreds of thousands of people gathered at the march. White people and black people are sitting together. Everyone is smiling and getting along.

Then Dr. King gets up to speak. He talks about his dream of freedom for everyone. He ends by quoting the spiritual, "Free at last, free at last. Thank God Almighty, we are free at last."

When you hear Dr. King speak and see all the people gathered at the march, you are hopeful too. Maybe you will not always worry about violence when you see a white person. Maybe peace will come to your city one day.

THE END

To follow another path, turn to page 11.
To read the conclusion, turn to page 101.

You head downstairs to see if any of your friends are there. BOOM! An explosion knocks out the windows and starts a fire. You are covered in shattered glass. You hear screaming. It is smoky, and you can't see.

You find the stair railing and follow it with your hand. As you reach the door, you hear a girl crying. "I can't see. I can't see. Help me!"

You yell, "The door's here. Come this way!" You grab the girl's hand and pull her out of the church. You are lucky to be alive. Four girls in the basement are not so lucky. They were killed by the blast of dynamite. You wonder if the United States will ever change. You hope that one day things will be different.

THE END

To follow another path, turn to page 11.
To read the conclusion, turn to page 101.

96

You stay inside and listen to the news reports. You make phone calls to your friends and feel better when you hear their voices. You wonder how much longer the violence will last. How much more will you have to go through to be treated fairly?

THE END

To follow another path, turn to page 11.
To read the conclusion, turn to page 101.

You need to be with your friends. You walk toward downtown and see your friend Johnny Robinson. You talk about the girls who were killed. Soon, a few other boys join you. Just then, some white boys drive by in a car decorated with Confederate flags. They roll down the windows and yell insults. You and your friends throw a few rocks at the car. It feels good to let out some anger.

You're turning around to leave when police officers show up. "Stop!" they yell. "Come over here right now." Johnny throws the last rock in his hand at the car. "Run!" you yell at him.

Johnny races off in one direction. You head the opposite way. The police go after Johnny as you run home as fast as you can. You think you hear a gunshot, but you keep going.

A few hours later, your parents ask to talk to you. "It's Johnny, son." You know it's not good news. "He's been killed."

The police shot Johnny in the back as he ran away. You know it could have been you. Your life seems hopeless. When, you wonder, will things change?

THE END

To follow another path, turn to page 11.
To read the conclusion, turn to page 101.

At least 250,000 people attended the March on Washington in August 1963.

CHAPTER 5

THE BATTLE FOR EQUALITY

School desegregation, Freedom Rides, and nonviolent protests were just a few of the civil rights battles. The movement inched along, one lunch counter at a time. One sports team at a time. One school. One store. One town. Hundreds of thousands of people took part in the effort for freedom and equal rights.

101

Turn the page.

The Freedom Riders of 1961 paved the way for Freedom Summer in 1964. That summer, members of the SNCC and other civil rights groups traveled to Mississippi. In that state, Jim Crow laws made it impossible for most African Americans to vote. Volunteers formed a new political party, the Mississippi Freedom Democratic Party. African Americans who joined the party were automatically registered to vote — 80,000 of them by the end of the summer.

But violence still haunted the civil rights movement. On June 21, 1964, three Freedom Summer volunteers disappeared near Philadelphia, Mississippi. On August 4, their beaten and shot bodies were found buried inside a dam made of earth. The killings went unsolved for more than 40 years.

Dr. Martin Luther King (second from right) was killed on the balcony of the Lorraine Motel.

April 4, 1968, was another terrible day for the movement. That evening, Dr. Martin Luther King Jr. was shot and killed as he stood on the balcony of a motel in Memphis, Tennessee. After his assassination, riots broke out across the country for a week.

Even so, the movement continued. The Civil Rights Acts of 1964 and 1968 gave African Americans equal chances at jobs and housing. The Voting Rights Act outlawed practices like poll taxes and literacy tests. Years later, killers were finally convicted in the cases of Medgar Evers, the Freedom Summer workers, and the Birmingham church bombing.

The civil rights movement helped African Americans move into positions of power. In 1967, Thurgood Marshall became the first African American Supreme Court justice. Recently, African Americans Colin Powell and Condoleeza Rice have served as U.S. secretary of state. In 2008, Barack Obama was elected the first African American president of the United States.

By 1964, African Americans were able to vote freely in elections.

Life is still not equal for all Americans. But the United States continues a commitment to change thanks to the civil rights movement.

Time Line

1954 — In *Brown vs. Board of Education of Topeka*, the U.S. Supreme Court rules that separate is not equal and segregation is illegal.

December 5, 1955 — The Montgomery, Alabama, bus boycott begins. It ends December 20, 1956.

September 1957 — Nine black students enroll at Central High School in Little Rock, Arkansas.

February 1, 1960 — Four African American college students stage a sit-in at a lunch counter in Greensboro, North Carolina.

April 17, 1960 — The Student Nonviolent Coordinating Committee (SNCC) is founded.

Summer 1961 — Freedom Rides take place to end segregation on public buses.

June 12, 1963 — Medgar Evers is assassinated in Decatur, Mississippi.

August 28, 1963 — At least 250,000 people participate in the March on Washington.

September 15, 1963 — A bomb explodes in the Sixteenth Street Baptist Church in Birmingham, Alabama, killing four young girls.

1964 — In June, three civil rights workers are murdered in Mississippi.

In July, Congress passes the Civil Rights Act of 1964.

1965 — Congress passes the Voting Rights Act.

April 4, 1968 — Dr. Martin Luther King Jr. is assassinated in Memphis, Tennessee. James Earl Ray later confesses to the crime.

In April, Congress passes the Civil Rights Act of 1968, which is also known as the Fair Housing Act.

1977 — Robert Chambliss is convicted for his role in the Sixteenth Street Baptist Church bombing.

1994 — Byron De La Beckwith is convicted of murdering Medgar Evers.

2001 — Thomas Blanton is convicted for taking part in the Sixteenth Street Baptist Church bombing.

2002 — Bobby Cherry is convicted for his role in the Sixteenth Street Baptist Church bombing.

2005 — Edgar Killen is convicted of planning the murder of the three Freedom Summer workers.

2008 — Barack Obama is elected president of the United States.

Other Paths to Explore

In this book, you've seen how the events surrounding the civil rights movement look different from three points of view.

Perspectives on history are as varied as the people who lived it. You can explore other paths on your own to learn more about what happened. Seeing history from many points of view is an important part of understanding it.

Here are some ideas for other civil rights movement points of view to explore:

+ Southern police officers often were ordered to mistreat African Americans. What would it have been like to be a police officer at that time?

+ Some southern African Americans moved north in search of a better life. What was life like for them?

+ Several civil rights workers were killed. What was it like knowing that your work for equality could get you killed?

READ MORE

Anderson, Dale. *Freedom Rides: Campaign for Equality.* Minneapolis: Compass Point Books, 2008.

Ingram, Scott. *The 1963 Civil Rights March.* Milwaukee: World Almanac, 2005.

Miller, Mara. *School Desegregation and the Story of the Little Rock Nine.* Berkeley Heights, N.J.: Enslow, 2008.

Supples, Kevin. *Speaking Out: The Civil Rights Movement, 1950–1964.* Washington, D.C.: National Geographic, 2006.

INTERNET SITES

FactHound offers a safe, fun way to find educator-approved Internet sites related to this book.

Here's what you do:

1. Visit *www.facthound.com*
2. Choose your grade level.
3. Begin your search.

This book's ID number is 9781429623452.

FactHound will fetch the best sites for you!

GLOSSARY

assassinate (us-SASS-uh-nate) — to murder a person who is well known or important

boycott (BOY-kot) — to refuse to buy or use a product or service in order to protest something believed to be wrong or unfair

desegregation (dee-seg-ruh-GAY-shuhn) — getting rid of any laws or practices that separate people of different races

integrate (IN-tuh-grate) — to bring people of different races together in schools and other public places

Ku Klux Klan (KOO KLUHX KLAN) — a group that promotes hate against African Americans and other groups; Ku Klux Klan members used violence to fight desegregation.

lynch (LINCH) — to put a person to death by hanging without a trial

paddy wagon (PAH-dee WAG-uhn) — a truck used by police officers to transport prisoners

segregation (seg-ruh-GAY-shuhn) — the policy of separating people according to their race

BIBLIOGRAPHY

Arsenault, Raymond. *Freedom Riders: 1961 and the Struggle for Racial Justice.* New York: Oxford University Press, 2006.

Bass, Patrik Henry. *Like a Mighty Stream: The March on Washington, August 28, 1963.* Philadelphia: Running Press, 2002.

Beals, Melba Pattillo. *Warriors Don't Cry: A Searing Memoir of the Battle to Integrate Little Rock's Central High.* New York: Pocket Books, 1994.

Boyd, Herb. *We Shall Overcome.* Naperville, Ill.: Sourcebooks, 2004.

Counts, Ira Wilmer. *A Life Is More Than a Moment: The Desegregation of Little Rock's Central High.* Bloomington, Ind.: Indiana University Press, 1999.

Halberstam, David. *The Children.* New York: Random House, 1998.

Jacoway, Elizabeth. *Turn Away Thy Son: Little Rock, the Crisis That Shocked the Nation.* New York: Free Press, 2007.

Williams, Juan. *Eyes on the Prize: America's Civil Rights Years, 1954–1965.* New York: Viking, 1987.

INDEX